GRAYSPACE

Carmen Vera

Order this book online at www.trafford.com
or email orders@trafford.com

Most Trafford titles are also available at major online book retailers.

Print information available on the last page.

ISBN: 978-1-4907-9587-4 (sc)
ISBN: 978-1-4907-9586-7 (e)

Library of Congress Control Number: 2019908502

Because of the dynamic nature of the Internet, any web addresses or links contained in
this book may have changed since publication and may no longer be valid. The views
expressed in this work are solely those of the author and do not necessarily reflect the views
of the publisher, and the publisher hereby disclaims any responsibility for them.

Our mission is to efficiently provide the world's finest, most comprehensive book publishing
service, enabling every author to experience success. To find out how to publish your book,
your way, and have it available worldwide, visit us online at www.trafford.com

Trafford rev. 07/01/2019

 www.trafford.com

North America & international
toll-free: 1 888 232 4444 (USA & Canada)
fax: 812 355 4082

Matt Parker, you have been the inspiration for the book. You continue to encourage me to be who I am. I will keep going. I will forever be in your corner.

Thank you, Kylie Brown, for the amazing book cover. You are so talented.

Thank you, Victoria Probert, for the beautiful author portrait. Your talent never ceases to amaze me.

Acknowledgments

Thank you mom and dad for giving me all tools I needed to succeed in life. I love you. You are so awesome.

Karyna Martinez, thank you for giving that push.

Kellie O'Toole, for continuously inspiring me and lending an ear.

Brown-Rosenson, nothing but love.

Stephany and Ali, for being my dream team, my Charlie's Angels, for encouraging me to write this.

Martyn, each day you continue to inspire me and keep me going. You are my personal coffee brew.

--And to all those bitches that tried to bury me, not knowing I was seed.

Foreword

I feel that I am a leprechaun holding onto this pot of gold! I want to share this gold with everyone! Sharing is caring. You become less of an asshole when you do too.

You've obviously picked up this book for your own reasons. It could be a few things. Whether it be because you are curious, you are genuinely trying to better yourself, or it was on clearance. Whatever it may be: Welcome!

We have all come from different walks of life. We will take all sorts of roads and paths. Sometimes we come to a fork in the road and we are unsure of what to do. We think of two options: Will I make the wrong choice? Or will I make the right choice? We tend to live in the black and white. It is one thing or the other. We can't have both.

I don't want want to say that I am a anarchist. BUT, I have definitely always been that type of person who has questioned and asked WHY? I have always wondered why things a *had* to be this or that--one thing or another. You can have vanilla or chocolate. I love both flavors. So, why can't I have both?

These were questions I asked myself. When I come up with an answer I realize there really isn't a good answer! And so that's when I decided to make a change in my life. I have accumulated a few key ideas that have been recurring themes in my life.

It took me a while to get to where I am at, but I can say that I'm truly happy and that's all anyone really wants, right (and puppies, too)? I learned that there is never a clear

one-and-done answer to anything. And people can be very uncomfortable without that solid answer. It *has* to be black and white. I'm here to preach that: NO IT DOESN'T.

Over time, I've developed 13 bullet points that have helped me live in that "in between" that we are all so uncomfortable with. All of these specific topics are meant to be easy, simple, and relatable. You will see the connection of all of these points in order in one way, and in many cases, all. I've gathered, organized, and plated it on a pretty platter for you in the form of a self help book named <u>Grayspace</u>.

I am now introducing the way I live. *I live in the gray.*

1. Don't be a sad bitch.

There are more ways than one solution to the problem. *Set realistic expectations, but be solution oriented.*

First things first. Ok, let's not beat around the bush. Life can sometimes suck ass. I'm not going to sit here and be unrealistic. I am not in the business of hiding the truth--and be weary of those who do try to hide it! Once we accept the reality that some really bad shit happens sometimes, it becomes a hair easier to swallow the truth. And this is where one should aim to set their expectations. You are allowed to have a positive mind frame. At the same time, be prepared that it will not always be a "perfect" life. The truth of the matter is: it doesn't exist. What you see on social media is not realistic. This is the highlight reel of someone's life. But what we do have power over is aiming for *your* perfect as possible for your own life.

It's a hit or miss. Sometimes it works. Sometimes it doesn't. You are allowed to be in touch with your emotions and be sad. But, do not be a sad bitch. What I mean from this is simple. You need to have a positive mindset and you cannot continue to mope around in sadness. It may seem that you are drowning when if you just stand up, you'll realize you've been in the shallow end this entire time. Point and case is to always be innovative. Find other ways to solve a situation. Be solution oriented and train your brain to be able to comprehend other ways to fix a problem.

This will sound a little confusing at first, but read on and I'll outline ways on how to find your own happiness and inner peace. You'll just need some good old fashioned practice and rewiring the thought process of the brain.

When you are unhappy and give into those feelings of helplessness, you are allowing yourself to be set up for failure. Take responsibility for yourself. Do not be upset when are you are creating your own storm cloud and being upset when it rains. "Misery loves company" is what it says. In a nutshell: you cannot enjoy your life when are you continuously in a rut where you are being sad. When you are not your best, you cannot live your life to the fullest. Also, who even likes to be sad? It's not a good feeling. If doesn't feel good, we're simply not here for it, y'all.

When you train your brain to be solution oriented. There is never one answer to every situation. And more than likely, you'll be running into problems quite often in this thing called life. You have the power to step back and take a moment to figure out how you will get it done. Trust yourself. Breathe. Take your time. You always have the option to do research and ask for help. Finding multiple solutions to a problem will give your mind the freedom. You will maintain a flexible mentality that will apply to many other aspects of your life.

Notes:

_____

_____

_____

_____

_____

2. Reset that mind.

I think good thoughts, I think good thoughts.

The law of attraction can be taken literally. It's there in the title. We attract what we want in life.

Take a moment. Take a breath. Close your eyes. Think about what you want. These examples include, but are not limited to: more money, a promotion at work, finding the love of your life, finding great friends, going on that dream vacation, etc. Sit there for a moment. Start with one good thing you want. Keep thinking about it. Take a breath, and think about why that thought is good. What will it bring you if you achieve that goal? If you get that promotion can you start to save up for that new house? Will you pay off some stubborn debt? Can you treat yourself to a nice spa day?

The point is: once we start to manifest happy and positive thoughts, *another* good thought will come after that. And then another one comes. And then another good thought, and so and so forth.

In turn, this can also happen with negative thoughts and spiral out of control quickly. "I'm never good enough." you say to yourself. And then it keeps perpetuating in a vicious cycle. You begin to think about every mistake you made in your life. You dwell on it even though you realize it's the past and there's nothing to do to change it. As humans, we all have qualms about what we could have done better. Learn to forgive yourself. Again, It's in the past. It has already happened. Refill your mind with positive thoughts. Learn from that mistake and move forward. We all make them. And spoiler alert: we will make them in the future too.

You're allowed to forgive. You're allowed to learn from it. And you're allowed to move forward.

Forgive yourself. Learn. Move forward. Lather. Rinse. Repeat.

Always remind yourself of the old saying: Fake it 'til you make it!

Confidence is key. The best part is no one will ever call you out on it because they'll never know. Use it to your advantage. Time to practice those acting skills. When your mind is confident, all else follows. When the mind is good, you are good. You're royalty now. Go, you!

Things that make me happy when I think about them:

_____

_____

_____

_____

_____

_____

_____

_____

_____

3. Spread the Love

"You are responsible for the energy that you create for yourself, and you're responsible for the energy that you bring to others." -Oprah Winfrey

(...And don't forget to bring the coffee!)

Point and case: YOU--and solely YOU--ARE RESPONSIBLE FOR ENERGY YOU BRING INTO YOUR CIRCLE. This means positive *and* negative energy. Cliches are there for a reason. They're true! They've been lived out a million times, and that should resonate within yourself. Other people have made this mistake before. They've learned from it, and so can you. You truly cannot love anyone else before you love anyone else.

Introducing negative people, ideas, and energy into your life will take a toll on you. This may not be immediate, but you'll start to see the effects over time. This is not sustainable for your mental health whatsoever. It may be "okay" for the time being, but you will allow yourself to be susceptible to the toxicity of others that does not grow you.

You'll begin to make excuses and convince yourself that it's going to be okay. That's not grayspace.

Let's be real. Everyone theoretically has a personal garden. The goal is to simply have a beautiful garden with lots of flowers. Some people just have dirt plots with manure. Either they are beginning to start something really good, or they just have literal cow poop. **Be weary of the difference, folks!** Our goal is to have as many pretty blossoming plants. We're not about gardens with no flowers. Do not plant seeds in people's gardens who you know will not water them.

Do not bring forth the energy of wanting someone to take care of your seeds when there's a possibility of them not taking care of it (This was not meant to be a pun on reproduction, but it also works for the parents reading). Use your own seeds to plant in your own garden. Use that energy for you, and watch your garden grow beautifully and wildy.

Anything negative wears at you as a person in whole. We can pretend to be and act strong. But for what? We're not training for the olympics (apologies if you are). What being strong is, is to be able to decide for yourself. "This is what I like. This is what I don't like. This is what I will engage in because it grows me, and this is what I will cut out because it doesn't do anything for me." You respect yourself to avoid anything that does not bring you happiness or peace. That is strength. **Strength is not suffering.**

I once had an old boss who taught me about the spaceship. You are the spaceship about to launch. Now, before a spaceship takes off, a lot of things are connected to it. But guess what? Once that space ship is ready for blast off, those things that are attached to it fall off naturally because of gravity. And that is comparative to the idea that once you shoot for the sky to achieve all you've wanting in this lifetime, all those negative items connected to you will naturally fall off. Those things cannot survive, and

will have to detach from you. Once you start doing big things for yourself, your circle will naturally form itself. You'll know whoever is meant to be there. Not everyone you will lose will be a loss.

I think of myself as a big coffee pot. I am a hot, freshly made, silver pot of yummy liquid goodness. I pour myself into other people's mugs. I continue to pour myself. People are loving the greatness of my taste. They want more. I pour more, of course, because I

love them. They are friends. They are family. I don't mind pouring to them because I can always refill myself. How, you ask? I refill myself with things that make me happy. I simply go back to brew. My job makes me happy. My dogs make me happy. My friends make me happy. Music makes me happy. There are so many things that bring me happiness that I do in my life so that I am continuously whole. That is how I am able to pour coffee onto others. I am continuously brewing all good things into my silver pot. At times, I feel that my pot will overflow quite often. And that's beautiful. The world can always use some more love.

On my bad days where I don't feel that I'm getting enough brew, my friends will even refill my pot with their brew or coffee I have poured for them before. We fill in where we need to. And that's the beauty of friendship.

There have been relationships in the past where some mugs I fill don't reciprocate refilling me. And yes, we still fill these cups because we are kind. We don't expect anything back. But when we continue to pour ourselves into mugs that do not return the favor, we begin to run out of coffee.

When your coffee supply continues to diminish you are unable to pour less and less coffee out to those to need it, and most importantly for yourself. The idea is to keep your coffee pot full so that you can give and give to people who do encourage, inspire, motivate you.

What fills my coffee pot?

_____

_____

_____

_____

_____

_____

_____

_____

_____

_____

_____

Whose coffee mug do I fill?

_____

_____

_____

_____

_____

_____

_____

_____

Who fills my coffee pot?

_____

_____

_____

_____

_____

_____

_____

_____

4. Know your worth.

Know what you bring to the table *and don't be afraid to sit alone.*

Be confident in knowing what you want, and don't be afraid to go after it. This is it, baby. You get one life to live. *That's it.* Let's put things in a bigger perspective. Dr. Ali Binazir breaks it down for us. The probability of you being alive is pretty much zero. Point and case directly from the horse's mouth:

The probability of you existing at all comes out to 1 in 10 2,685,000—
yes, that's a 10 followed by 2,685,000 zeroes!

This literally means you have more of a chance to win the lottery ten times versus being alive. You have been given a sacred gift. Enjoy the gift *immensely*! Give it your best and live life the way you want to and how you've always dreamed to. Cut anyone and anything out of your life that has told you that you are less than or undeserving of something. You genuinely don't need that. It's unnecessary. We're working with the essentials. You'll be 100% better off and relieved after you shut out people who no longer grow you. It'll feel like a breath of fresh air from the Swiss mountain tops.

Many of us come from different backgrounds and walks of life. Some of us are not as privileged as others. It's very important to know where you came from and understand it. But do not make yourself a product of that environment if it's negative. Break the cycle. This can be painful as expected. Though we know it is crucial that it needs to end. This is a journey in itself to reprogram your mind and thought process. This will take time. Do not rush yourself.

Repeat the mantra over and over again. You are important. You are strong. And you are most definitely worth it--and you CAN do it.

5. Birds of a feather flock together.

Your support system is essential in succeeding and maintaining a life of genuine happiness. Often times we are afraid to end relationships in fear of the unknowing. Even though they are negative, we fear that losing them will be a loss. In reality, if a person doesn't radiate positive energy in you life, it's time to get rid of them. Thank people for their time if they no longer continue to grow you.

Many successful people will agree that in order to achieve success, you'll need to surround yourself with those that are like minded. Just like the law of attraction, you'll begin to manifest good, positive energy if your inner circle is a solid one. In turn, if you're consistently hanging out with the wrong group of people, they will more than likely bring you down--or worse. Continuing to surround yourself with that group can leave you stagnant and result in feelings of confusion and idle. That negative energy is undeserving of your time.

You are as tall as the shoulders you stand on. Learn to walk away from those who no longer contribute in your life. There are people that are meant to be in your life to teach you lessons. They are not meant to stay for your entire life's journey. Your life is a movie-- and you're the star. They play their supporting role and that's it. You must teach

yourself to let go because, again, not every person you lose is a loss. Thank that person for their time and move on. Make room for new people in your life. You'll clean house and open yourself to more life experience and make awesome memories. The cycle will repeat. Be aware.

We oftentimes have the tendency of wanting to fix people and their problems. We want to help. But we can't help others until we help ourselves first. We must come to the realization that we need to allow toxic people to be toxic on their own. The hardest pill to swallow is accepting the fact that you cannot live your life for other people. You want those in your life to live their best lives because you are looking from the outside in. You then wonder why they don't take your advice. It's best to leave them be. They must live life for themselves. "You can only lead a horse to water, but cannot make them drink it."

Just because you cut someone off doesn't mean that they will become enemies. You still want them to eat. You just cannot allow them to sit alongside you at your table.

Who are the people who love me unconditionally?

_____

_____

_____

_____

_____

_____

6. GRAY SPACE

There's black and white. And then there's gray space. Life is a ever revolving door, nothing lasts forever. Learn to love the gray.

Life is never a sure thing. Think of life as a ever revolving door. There is a color spectrum with black being one end, and the white being on the other end. Most are comfortable with living in either the black or white. That is what we perceived to be a "perfect" life. That is what we strive for. This is a dream. Of course we all wish we could have that perfect life that are portrayed in films. But we have to go back to the mentality of realistic expectations. Contrary to popular belief, we shouldn't want to be on the extreme ends of the spectrums. There needs to be a balance of both.

Life is not easy. And to get to where you want to go will be a long journey. Though we love instant gratification, it's simply not feasible or realistic. Good things take time to mature. Just like plants, they start as a seed. Then they become bigger, stronger. Where you will want to be takes time. Most of your journey will be in the gray spectrum having the combination of both the black and the white. Life will have its ways of throwing obstacles at you. Be prepared to expect the unexpected.

7. Ask for help.

Don't be scared to ask for help. Make that inner circle of friends a solid super system

SOS! Remember that game Who Wants to be a Millionaire? The contestant had the opportunity to choose 3 lifelines if they did not know the answer to the question. The good news is, you don't have only 3 opportunities. You have unlimited lifelines!

Reach out to those you love and trust. In turn, you may need to pick them up on another day too. It takes two oars to row a boat. You can both take turns rowing in order to continue to move forward. As The Beatles once famously said, "I get by with a little help from my friends."

If you're unsure and feel that you don't have anyone to speak to, therapists are available. You may even remain anonymous if you feel uncomfortable about your situation.

All in all, help is out there in the most various of ways. Sometimes we have to search for them and find a way that works for our respective situations. There are countless outlets to relieve your stress. Some examples are, but are not limited to: calling a friend, music, writing, dancing, art, fitness, gardening, photography, reading, cooking, baking, coloring, hiking, movies, and so, so much more! The possibilities are endless. Remember, though you may feel like it, you are never alone. This should comfort you that humans all experience similar problems.

When I'm feeling down, I (do):

_____

_____

_____

_____

_____

_____

_____

_____

8. Self Care

A little self care never hurt no one. Put on that face mask!

Self care differs from vanity. We are taught to put others before us. What we don't realize is that if we, ourselves, aren't good--the people around us can't be good either. It is crucial that we take time for ourselves to make us happy. Personally, I love getting my hair and nails done. There is nothing like a fresh trim, and a new manicure. And it's not just a myth. When you look good, you feel good! Take care of yourself and your confidence will grow wildly. Don't be afraid to splurge on yourself every once and awhile. If you are worried about money, you will need to find out budget or more affordable options for yourself. For example, if weekly manicures are something you like, try and learn how to do it on your own. YouTube is a wealth of DIY tutorials. At the same time, you'll learn a cost effective skill set and at the same time you will be treating yourself. Get yourself into the routine and restore some structure in your life. You will thank yourself in the long run.

Exercise

Yuck! Wouldn't you rather wash your mouth out with chocolate when you hear that word? Exercise seems like an unattainable goal. I'm here to tell you it's not.

What kind of physical activities do you like? Do you have a sport that you played in your youth? Do you like more scenic ways of exercise? Do you like hiking? Something low impact like swimming? Do you like having a class with an instructor that gives you structure? Do you like something independent or do you like playing with a team?

The trick is we disguise our exercise into something we like. Simply signing up for a gym membership won't give you the structure you need and won't hold you accountable. You'll just be wasting money. Let's say you don't know what you like. This is the perfect time to explore and see what will challenge and grow you. Ever gone to a broadway performance and have been mesmerized by the ballet dancers? You too can take up ballet. Ever want to learn how to protect yourself from danger? Take a self defense or boxing class. Your options are literally endless. Find an activity or two that you know you will like. You'll set goals and keep getting better. And who says you can't bring a friend along with you? That's the best part!

How I work out:

_____

_____

_____

New workout methods I'd like to try:

_____

_____

_____

_____

_____

Big sight goals:

_____

_____

_____

Diet

Research, research, research. Not every diet is going to work for everyone. If you have the opportunity, consult a physician to see what you can do to reach a healthy weight and lifestyle. Read up on the kind of diet you want to have in your life. Careful not to deprive yourself of anything. This is all a gradual process. This is the gray space. Be comfortable with the transitional period to give your mind and body time it needs. Fad diets and influencers will talk about the end results, but that's not realistic. We need to look into the transitional period because that is what most everyone faces challenges with. More often than not, you will continue to be in the gray for quite some time. Be comfortable with being uncomfortable. You **can** do this!

What kind of diet am I aiming for:

_____

I will get there by:

_____

_____

_____

_____

Planning
"Failing to plan is planning to fail."

Set your life up with a solid foundation and have a gameplan. Think about your future in regards to your retirement and pension. Do want to contribute 10% of every paycheck into your 401k? Will you set aside 'x' amount of dollars to your savings account? Make sure that you are taken care of at the end of your life. Do you have assets? Set aside time to create a will to make sure all your values and properties are left to the right person. There are no blurred lines. A lawyer can help with this. Things can get messy when money is involved. If you can, hire a professional fiduciary to take care of all your estate. When there are no emotional attachments, your loved ones can move on without the unnecessary litigation and costs of the courts.

Getting life insurance is something that needs to be to be stressed over and over. There are countless Gofundmes, pizza parties, and car washes that happen so that a family can pay for funeral arrangements for a person. Do not put this burden on your family. Once you find a policy that suits your needs, you'll realize that life insurance very affordable. This will take off any pressure if any unexpected tragedies happen.

At the end of the day, you'll have a set up from this point of your life forward. You'll know what will happen and you won't worry when you plan in advance. It seems scary at first, but once you get to the nitty gritty of these uncomfortable situations, you'll be thankful. You can go to bed at night and know for a fact that your loved ones will be taken care of and in turn, you will be too.

I need to take care of:

_____due by:_____
_____due by:_____
_____due by:_____
_____due by:_____

Big picture goals:

_____
_____
_____
_____
_____
_____
_____

Notes:

_____
_____

_____

_____

Therapy

Heck! These guys went to college for this! Feel free to pull a professional into this to talk out your frustrations or overwhelming issues in your life. These guys are here to help you. Utilize these resources.

THINGS THAT MAKE YOU HAPPY. Do them!

What makes you happy? Do you have a hobby you like or want to take up? Try new things or go back to the old. Start seeking interests and let your mind expand and grow you. Do you like to travel and learn about new cultures? Take a trip every once in a while. Keep your mind a sponge and let it soak up all the world has to offer.

Things I like to do:

_____

_____

_____

_____

_____

_____

_____

_____

_____

9. Speak up!

Be loud and proud about this! Even if your voice is shaking--say what you want, and say what you mean! There is also the last step of this in which many forget and that is to follow through. You need to have the self discipline to make sure that what is said comes to fruition.

I once had a friend who would say one thing. I'd do it. Then she'd get upset with me for not doing what she *really* wanted despite the fact she said the opposite of what she truly wanted. I would feel guilty, but for what? I'm not in the business of mind reading. That's not my fault. That's when I realized why in the hell do we not just say what we truly want? When I have been blatantly honest about the things I've wanted, I was able to achieve my dreams without any sugar coating or bull. This is such a simple, and *EASY*

concept. It's effortless to add it into your thought process. Allowing yourself that freedom to choose will alleviate a lot of stress. Also, it's sexy. A person who knows exactly what they want is an attractive quality. Your friends will love you for it. It's a win-win.

You're allowed to call the shots. You're allowed to keep editing your life. It is your very own masterpiece after all.

10. Be honest like Abe

You owe it to yourself to speak the truth. My dad had always taught me, "If you don't lie, you don't have anything to remember." When you are honest and upfront you allow yourself to really get to know what your wants and needs are. Covering things up is not a sustainable lifestyle. You'll always be seeking another high or unhealthy outlet to justify your actions. Telling the truth is the best thing you can do for yourself. Otherwise, you can create terrible habits for yourself always going back and retracing your steps. We want to aim for a life of simplicity. And that simplicity comes from living your truth.

We all have dirty laundry. We can choose to air it out publicly, or deal with it on our own. The truth is everyone has that dirty laundry pile. You will decide what to do with it. You can donate, wash, or throw away your clothes. There's no time frame on this and you can deal with this when you are ready. Others have cleaner closets than some because they've decided to deal with their dirty laundry head on. At the end of the day, there is no deadline, but dealing with things sooner or later will benefit you and you should try to make a tentative goal.

And let's be honest, pun intended--the truth will always come out whether it's now or later. It's inevitable.

Dirty Laundry and their due dates:

_____

_____

_____

_____

_____

_____

_____

_____

_____

_____

11. Balance, boundaries, limits, and the hard no.

Some things need to be in the black and white. It isn't always gray ironically.

You're not peanut butter. Be sure that you're not spreading yourself too thin. We have energy that we bestow onto others. The part in which we hold responsibility in is that we must decide who receives that energy. Saying no is difficult, and it feels uncomfortable. Once you get the hang of it, you'll reap all the benefits.

Just like a weighing scale, you'll need balance in your life. Go to work yes, but also allow yourself the time to play. Having one alongside the other will help you maintain this balance. Just like yin and yang, they must coexist together.

You are allowed to say no. If you ever feel uncomfortable or need a mental day, tell the person. Be upfront with them. If you need little time to yourself to regroup, or simply need a day to lay in bed and watch movies, you're allowed to say no. That's it. Just say no. Don't think about it. You know yourself and your limits better than anyone else. Someone who is a friend will understand and won't question you twice.

12. Time is your friend

Ah, time. That son of a bitch.

You can't start over. You can't. No matter how much you wish that you could do differently, it's not going to happen. We fantasize a lot a society. We have this idea that time can be frozen, or we could go back thanks to the creation of movies and television. But that's all Hollywood--not real life. Think about it. Just because things could have been different, doesn't mean they could have been better than they are now.

Though time can hurt us, we can also use it to our advantage. Time will heal or make tragedy manageable. Only time will tell what we're ultimately destined to do and where we end up. Looking back on things we analyze situations and think "Hm, that wasn't so bad. I wondered why I stressed out. Everything turned out fine." As long as your foundation is strong and you are prepared, there's no need to worry. The power of the mind will allow you to overcome any and all obstacles. Now that you have realistic expectations, you can conquer anything. Though tragedy strikes, we never realize how strong we are when we have to be. Especially in the face of our children or loved ones, we have to put on a strong front.

Life is uncertain. The only thing that's certain in life is uncertainty.

13. The little things.

Enjoy. Enjoy. Enjoy. ENJOY.

Don't take things so seriously. And one more time for those in the back: Don't take things so seriously. Once, someone told me that I shouldn't take things so seriously because I won't make it out alive. And it didn't click for me until I became an adult.

The stars and universe have aligned to create exactly--YOU! From the top of your head to the bottom of your toes, you have been created. You're literally made up from star stuff, the universe is in you, and you're in the universe. Your atoms were forged in the hearts of stars, they've journeyed space and time to make you. The chances that you are here to exist in the here and now are vast and the percentage is in the billions. Even from the time you were conceived, the chance of you winning the sperm race was small. But you--you made it! Be proud of that! Be proud of who you are. You call the shots, and you are meant to live the life you've always wanted. You're well deserving of the life you were destined to live.

That's the big picture. In the smaller picture, you're allowed to enjoy the little things. You like to take your walk in the morning? You like that special brand of mayonnaise at the store? You like your laundry done with a specific detergent? Yes, enjoy it. These little victories make life enjoyable. Take time to enjoy each of those little moments of happiness in your day to day life.

Random things that make me happy:

_____

_____

_____

_____

_____

_____

_____

_____

_____

_____

_____

_____

14. The Carnival

The carnival of life—and you can win every time!

Carnivals! Ahhh, the smell of the crisp summer night. It's a little humid, but not too much. There they are. The bright lights illuminating the corn dogs, burgers, funnel cake signs. There are so many food options you can't read them all at once. There's so much to take in as you hear the live music from the band. You look left there are carnival

rides. You look to the right. There are games. There's a man yelling, "Step right up!" as he challenges the next player to take a sledgehammer and hit the bottom of a bell to win a big stuffed animal. There's a huge crowd. You see people smiling and laughing. Some are walking around with their beers. There you are stood right in the middle of it all. You look up. You see the big ferris wheel with all the lights.

Your life can be compared to a carnival. Whatever you decide to put into your carnival should be catered to you. What games are you putting in your carnival? These games are going to be rigged to where you can win a prize *every single time*. There's no reason to why you should put a game in where you lose every time--and you don't have to! You fill this carnival with whatever your heart desires. Yes, whatever you wish. What kind of food do you like? Are you going to put your favorite foods? Or are you going to stick with something healthier. What beverages are you serving? Who is at your carnival when you look around? Is it your family and friends joining you in the festivities?

You look around and see all the favorite rides you've put inside. You then go up to the ferris wheel. You look up. It's big and beautiful with bright lights. It's your turn to get into the car. The wheel takes you up. You finally get to the top. You look down at your carnival. Do you like what you see when you look down? What is going through your mind? What music is playing in the background? Who else is on the ferris wheel and who is sitting next to you? Are you happy with what you see?

Printed in the United States
By Bookmasters